Paradise Is Jagged

Also by Ann Fisher-Wirth

The Bones of Winter Birds
Mississippi (with Maude Schuyler Clay)
Dream Cabinet
Carta Marina
Five Terraces
Blue Window

The Ecopoetry Anthology (coedited with Laura-Gray Street)

*William Carlos Williams and Autobiography: The Woods
of His Own Nature*

Paradise Is Jagged

Ann Fisher-Wirth

Terrapin Books

Terrapin Books
4 Midvale Avenue
West Caldwell, NJ 07006

www.terrapinbooks.com

ISBN: 978-1-947896-60-4
Library of Congress Control Number: 2022946389

First Edition
Redux Series

Cover art by Irma Randall Mitchell
North Mississippi
oil on canvas
37" X 48"

Cover design by Diane Lockward

Contents

for Jennifer

A Young Stag at Dusk

White tail flicking, eating flowers
heaped on a raw grave,

he raises his head to watch us
before he vanishes slowly into the trees.

~

Outside the kitchen window,

my Peace roses ride on arching stems
like moons in a lead-white sky.

—*My?* All year, earth holds them,
I ignore them.

~

Night thickens among the branches

of gingko, maple, willow oak, cherry,
redbud, and the thicket of bamboo

that surround this wooden house.
Sometimes I am afraid.

~

At three I knelt on the back seat

of my mother's car and, looking out the window,
said, *There's so much to see*

and so little time to see it. Or so I've been told.
It's like that now, watching the leaves.

~

Bread rises in the oven.

May the stag sink back into the forest.
May the petals drop on the grass.

Whoever you are, may you be at peace
in this great silence, where only the birds speak.

One

Imagining Caroline Casper.
Nebraska 1880

Her sons were so lithe and quick,
racing with salt to catch the tail feathers of birds.
They even laughed when they fell.
And the whole bright sky around them,
every branch and leaf in that high windy arch,
shook like gypsy tambourines against the blue.

But she was a woman. Dressed in brown
or blue, she worked by the kitchen window.
No lover came to meet her,
no white feather drifted down
from Canada geese as they soared screaming
in leave-taking above the stinging water,

the whole wintry flight of them strong and fierce
and free. Yes, she was a woman and her level blue eyes
left no mark unnoticed on the table.
Her hands learned to be quick at gathering fruit
or sewing seams or plucking the feathers
from birds. Home was her church, and she the arch—

for women are the keystone, the preacher said.
Her whole life, she learned pleasure was flimsy
as feathers. Like rivers she could not travel,
the thick blue veins rose up in her hands. Her nails

broke to the quick. Up to the elbows in work,
she could not leave.

But once, as she stood washing, great dark leaves
began to sway outside the window.
Her back pricked as if somebody watched her.
Drying her hands, she turned.
The whole sky darkened. From the shadows,
a deeper blue gathered up in a rustle of feathers.

Sunday, a Zuihitsu

Clumps of snow falling across the window as sun comes to the branches of the willow oak. I'm lying in bed mid-afternoon with my beloved, too cold to get up, my feet like chunks of ice, his skin so warm. The snow in clusters caught by light like white petals, and the scatter-sound as they hit the deck. In a slither of fur, one fat squirrel running up the trunk, dodging.

I'm thinking about my Nebraska-born mother. She rarely smiled. Instead, her habit was pleasant—but in the French sense, *plaisant*, not only pleasant, but pleasing. When I wish I believed in an afterlife, it's so she could know how much I loved her. She overcooked vegetables, put too much salt on popcorn. Her salads were iceberg lettuce with radish slices and bottled dressing that burned your lips.

My mother would have painted what I see—the sky faint pink as dusk settles through the trees, snow still lining the branches, darker pink of a few remnant quince petals, pinpoints of light and a slash of white roof down the hill. She would have painted the scratch-scratch, the every-which-way-ness of branches, with the light and air surrounding them. Watching her, I would have been drawn to her silence.

The Oakland Art Museum asked her for paintings but she refused. When, years later, I showed her my poems, she told me, *These are beautiful but the soul is like a crystal goblet, easily shattered by the world. You must never publish*. Yet, later still, when she had to enter assisted living, she tried to sell her portraits in a yard sale, and nobody bought them. *No one has ever cared two hoots about my art*, she said.

My house is full of her paintings. My children's houses are full of her paintings. My sister's house, her children's houses. Every time I lie in bed I gaze at two of her paintings.

—All these things held together in the weave of Sunday, and memories of Christian Science—sitting in Sunday School, admiring my white scallop-edged cotton gloves with the little petal cutouts, rising to sing the hymns each week. And I believed if Jesus could walk on water, I could too.

Sex, I thought, was when two grownups lay at opposite ends of a bed with their legs in a V and scooted up till their bottoms touched. Couldn't imagine my parents would do that. They slept in mahogany rose-carved twins, but once or twice I woke them up and found them snuggling, she in a white lacy nightgown, he in saggy Balbriggan pajamas.

Make your beds, do your homework, sit up straight, set the table, mind your manners. *Mabel Mabel sweet and able / keep your elbows off the table.* Ann wash, Jennifer dry. Both of you run along now, take your baths and say your prayers.

Her body was our safety. Singing voice like slender water. Hands with almond-shaped fingernails softly scratching our backs. "God is Love," she told us, "and you are His perfect child."

All those years when he was at war, she wrote him every day. Who were they? My mother soft, my father stiff in his Army uniform. Their devotion. She said to me once, *When you've lived through war, all you want is a family.* We clung to her. She had to keep shooing us outside to play.

I woke her up one night. *I'm afraid of something that starts with D.*
Daddy?
No.
Dogs?
No.
She was quiet a moment, thinking. She put her arms around me.
Death?

Childhood

How soft were her hands, stroking
our hair as she sang to us,
my little sister and me—lullabies
that curved through the silvery trees.

Our father was somewhere
called Korea. He wrote to us
that children in crimson overalls
ran after him for American candy.

Now I know that suffering
sows the earth with salt,
but then I only wondered
how the birds slept, feathers

puffed out around them
in the darkness, what frogs said
with their burbling throats,
where the mysterious rivers ran.

Outside Sagamihara

Blue irises
　　　　in a bucket
　　　　　　　　beside a rutted
　　　　　road
muddy　puddles
　　　　the one-room
　　　　　　　　shop so fragile
　　　　as if made of
matchsticks and
　　　　the woman
　　　　　　　　young　or old
　　　　I do not know　I was
a child　my mother
　　　　picked her way
　　　　　　　　from the green
　　　　Ford across
the puddles into
　　　　the shop to buy
　　　　　　　　irises　this was
　　　　Japan　1954
this was war's
　　　　long reach of
　　　　　　　　poverty

no other flowers
　　　　only
　　　　　　　　blue irises

I Want to Be a Gladiola

but I'm chubby, thirteen, my braces just came off
and my mother plucked my eyebrows.
I've curled my hair and put on Tangee lipstick
and the bottle green taffeta tulip skirt dress
I made my mother buy me
for dinner with our relatives. I am the epitome
of glamour, the *ne plus ultra* of seething flesh
in this cocktail dress for a 30-year-old,
and I goo-goo-eye the waiter, ready to elope with him
to the wilds of Colorado.
Meanwhile the aunt we've never met
asks my sister and me if we miss Japan,
how we like California, and our uncle, the rich lawyer,
grills our father, *So, what's next,*
now that you're finished with the Army?
1960, Beverly Hills, a place I hadn't heard of,
everybody coolly glittering.
I chew my shrimp and sip my Shirley Temple
above a breathless pit called you'll-never-find-love.
My *coupe glacée* arrives.
My Merry Widow's pinching.
My garter belt makes welts on the backs of my thighs.

Ironing

. . . you have the whole of space and time / to find the face you seek.
— "To a Diver," Gyorgyi Voros

We're sending our father his Christmas box —
first and second-grade pictures,
a gray flannel shirt, fleece-lined slippers, stinky cheese —
It's cold in Korea, our mother tells us, *and he misses*
food from home. We blow kisses in the box,
wrap it with twine,
seal each seam with melted wax,
and off it goes to his APO.

    Next, it's time for ironing.
We press handkerchiefs at our own small boards
as she deftly noses her iron into the gathers of skirts,
smooths out collars and lapels,
lines up pleats and holds them firm
while with the iron she slicks the steam in.

The kitchen becomes a fragrant cave,
full of the week's fresh clothes
hanging from the cupboard knobs.
And as we follow our father
from Pennsylvania to Japan, from Japan
to California, we while away the work
with "Let's Describe" or "Movie Stars" —
Let's describe a ballgown, let's describe

a beach cabana—Can you name three
movie actresses whose last names start with C?

~

     Now, as the wind rises,
I smooth and press the lace-edged cutwork napkins
that she folded next to the rose chintz Spode
when she hosted Army wives.

And I recall the chapel—my navy blue wool dress,
my fear to touch his face,

one bronze chrysanthemum petal
falling on his hand. Our mother telling the undertaker,
Let me fix his hair.
He never wore it parted quite so high.

Freedom's Just Another Word

Telegraph, 1963: before the Angels
rode through on their hogs and started dealing,
the summer Susie Cahill and I pulled on our black tights
and fishnet sweaters, lined our eyes like Cleopatra,
and strolled down the hill
with our rhinestone pipes and Latakia.

    A bas! to my high school social club,
    Adelphians, second coolest at Berkeley High,
    à bas! to my girdle and kitten heels,
    even my mom couldn't make me go sit
    in a circle and—what did we do?
    eat cupcakes, talk about hair and Frankie Avalon?—
    à bas! to dances at the Brazil Room
    up at Tilden, where wind blew through the eucalyptus
    and I shivered in my scarlet sheath,
    pink carnation wrist corsage
    draped listless over my boyfriend's shoulder.

You could nurse a caffè latte
at the Mediterraneum, where the espresso machine
steamed and sputtered, and Julia Vinograd,
famous "Bubble Lady" of People's Park,
trailed through the café in her velvet
tasseled cap and floor-length skirt,
selling her stapled poetry chapbooks for one dollar,

and the beautiful guy with the shock of wheat-scorched hair
held forth from his table about love.

He drew my profile in green ink,
leafy tendrils weaving around me and up from my hair.
I followed him to his mattress on the floor.
Next morning, cold spaghetti from an iron pot—
and when I passed him later by Cody's,
he started singing "Pretty Woman."

> Back to high school, the breathless boredom,
> the silent house,
> and mother grieving.

Fraught Season

Once again, birds parcel out the sky.

I want to feel how their songs are gifts

and the leggy pansies, running to seed
near the end of their season,
and the three strawberries I've managed to grow,

each partly rotted or eaten,

the snapdragons and dianthus, mint,
the orangey pink geranium, marigolds, lantanas,
raindrops dripping from the eaves,

the squirrel that just skittered across the yard

and ran up the crepe myrtle, the *sloosh* of cars
driving down the wet street—and a memory,
so early I don't even know if it's true—

myself, lying in a cot in a hotel, watching

the blurred reflection of streetlights in the window
as their lozenges of color changed, hearing
that same wet *sloosh*—the mystery that surrounds us,

the otherness of lives passing on the night street

as I lay cocooned in my parents' love,
in the lights, the rain—and now here,
the battered sun,

the fine mesh and delicate tracery of leaves

on trees so huge they blot out the white sky.

Komm süßer Tod

Come sweet death, my sister wrote in her secret notebook
at thirteen, shortly after our father died. *Come,
sweet death, for I grow weary of my living.*

*I am a tumbling stream
that burbles over rocks and swerves around boulders,
but at last falls silent when it spreads to meet the ocean.*

Snooping, I read what she wrote.
I had no words for how he lingered, then collapsed,
how his brown and pink plaid laprobe
held the smell of his decay—

now evil seeds keep scattering through her body.
I keep wanting to tell our mother, long since dead,
She's sick, she needs you, go to her quickly.

And Behind Us, Only Air

Ten days from death, she glows, sitting beside me
on their deck, scarf wrapped around her head.

She's leaning toward me. I have a cold
so I'm leaning away, afraid to give her

one more thing to fight, and it hurts
that someone seeing this photograph

might think I'm avoiding her. She's softly
smiling at the photographer—her husband—

on this my last visit. I feel messy,
unfinished; there's too much of me,

I'm too given over to life, and all that has
been stripped from her. She has gone

beyond grief. Not yet is she skeletal, quite.

Inhabitation

A year ago midsummer, we visited Magnolia Grove,
you with your newly shaved head, and when
I introduced you, Sister Boi and Sister Peace,
likewise bald, embraced you.
                              Heat gathers,
every day hotter than the day before.
Something lives in our walls again,
scrabbling behind the bricked up fireplace,
and ants spill out from infinitesimal cracks
in the corners. Apricots rot before they're ripe.
My days in near seclusion
creep through the hours and surrender to sleep.
Or to twitches, as if I'm a rag doll shaken.

                    ~

I can't tell you how I miss you.
I keep wanting to phone you,
ask something you would know,
with your flawless memory—
what year our father went to Korea,
when and how our grandparents died.
To ask if you remember all that past—
But one night, as I lay there twitching,
trying to sleep, you came
through the shining membrane
between life and death, so that I saw you,

and I *was* you, gaunt edifice, cage of bone,
and the clear, diminishing flame
that was still, in that second, my sister.

Persimmons

My sister said, *I would like to write*
about these persimmons but I can't.

Along the street they hung,
glossy and taut among the leaves,

all of light in their red-orange flesh,
like breasts, like buttocks or wombs

swollen with sun, with desire,
those sexy fruits that she loved,

on this radiant All Souls' morning
when she returned to walk with me.

Namesake

It's 1965. In a spill of light
a girl sits on a bed cross-legged,
trimming split ends from her hair.
She pulls each blonde strand
around, squints at it, the little
curved blades of the scissors
snip, snip, the hairs fall
on her sweater, in her lap.
She's so lonely and bored,
freshman year and far from home,
it's Illinois, and winter.
Snow and endless darkness.
She has learned about the abyss
and she thinks, *snip, snip*,
she might be at the edge of the abyss.

                    ~

Someone comes to get her for the phone.
I see it though I never saw it,
down the hall, rotary, black,
on a scuffed table. Her mother
has called from California,
her sister has had the baby
and named it after her.
Jennifer Lisa. Her heart blazes—
this namesake she will
never see, this illegitimate baby
who will soon be given away.

~

That, more or less, is the story
my sister wrote
for English her freshman year
and showed me many years later.
In her story, the baby lives,
and the girl returns to sit on her bed.
Snip, snip. A child has been named
for her. It's a secret, but it glows.

~

In my actual, silent family, we never
mentioned my stillborn child.
But when I think of my sister, now dead,
or when I think of the child
whom I did name Jennifer Lisa,
sometimes from the dark
muck of suffering, joy rises
like the lotus flowers
my sister and I beheld
the summer of her last illness,
completely covering the pond where we walked,
white and pale golden above their leaves.

Two

Postcard of an Anonymous Wooden Carving

Oh child, little toes extending
from your stiff carved robes,
orb with the cross in one hand,
other hand raised in benediction.
Your overlarge head and mild wide eyes.
Here you are calm, in this narrow alcove.
Suffering is not yet. A light pours down
around you. Run outside and see
if the peaches are ripening on the trees,
see if the lambs in the fields skip sideways.

Meditation Facing into Rain

—in the California mountains

Misty sunlight, and the creeks
            full, land that was parched
      and cracked four months ago
green as a dream

                  redwoods
duff and crumble underfoot

and the hairy lichens that look like Spanish moss
                  drowned witches' hair
      tufts caught on the tips of live oaks

always I am at peace here
            in this silence
                  and the sound of water

      look at the twist and gnarl of live oak
branches spreading, twisting
      all the way back to the ground

            we begin how we begin

my son is becoming a father
            the doors of his life swing open in the wind
and the whole frame trembles

Winter Day on the Whirlpool Trails

Where the power lines go through,
the red clay gullies and pits, not even
privet can grow fast enough to bind it.
We clamber down and up,
and turn to enter the woods. Farther along,
we come to broken glass, old brown bottles
nearly buried, a toilet choked with brush,
bricks, some pipes, some turquoise plastic coiling.
It's just like that, here—people dump things
and they sink, protrude rusty and jagged
from the mud, or block the trail,
stained with leaf mold. To the side,
some withered Southern red oaks,
a blackjack oak, knobby trunks of trees
choked by spiraling vines—Virginia creeper,
poison ivy—and leafless sweet gums
with their sci-fi seedpods.
Everywhere rotting, everywhere teeming,
moss like emeralds on the stumps
and hollow logs. This is my home, this leaf duff
and dereliction, where a vulture wheels
above the cedars, searching for what stinks.
Where a first tender violet, blooming
by my feet before Valentine's Day,
signifies the seasons are in heat.
The great blue heron's not here today,

standing motionless among the reeds.
But a turtle slides off a distant log, and sunlight
scatters like shot across the scum-slicked pond.

Late May

I'm on my deck in my underwear,
  starved for sunlight.
     Without people,
   the sky is clean again,
and all day long
   the birds clamor and musick.
      A woodpecker drills
   at a telephone pole,
and two cardinals dive bomb each other
   through the privet.
      A world empty of people,
    just uninterrupted grass,
Lawrence wrote a hundred years ago,
   and a hare sitting up,
      ready to bound,
   alert and quivering.
Nowhere to go, nothing to do,
   the monks and nuns sing,
     standing in a circle
   beneath the trees
at Magnolia Grove,
   Thich Nhat Hanh's monastery
     in Mississipppi,
   and today I'd like to sit
with Sister Boi and Sister Peace,
   eat vegetables and tofu,
     then wash my plate and bowl

in the series of pans—
dirty water, soapy water,
rinse water, clear. Like this sky,
like the breeze in which
the daylight swims.

Catalpa

This tree is older than Columbus. Ten years ago my honors students standing in a ring could barely get their arms around it. I took their picture—hands joined, cheeks against the rough wood. Mostly they loved it, but one guy told my friend who supervised his lab, *She made us hug a tree. It was the worst class ever*.

When I think of the tree as a sapling, my mind enters a great quiet. Before the Depression, the yellow fever, before the burning of Oxford, before the University Greys left their classrooms for the battlefield and died or were wounded to a man at Pickett's Charge, and before Princess Hoka of the Chickasaws set out with her people on the Trail of Tears, this tree sank its roots deep and deeper into the ground. Generations moved about beneath its boughs, spoke and loved and died as it grew.

And here it is, still, in the clattering present.

Ten years ago I could walk around it, smell it, stroke the lichen on its bark. If I put my hand into the hollow in its trunk right near the ground, it was always cold, always comforting. No matter how brutal the summer, its dark, mysterious lungs kept serenely breathing.

Now fences surround it, stakes hold up its branches. No longer do art majors loll on the benches and smoke under its big-leaf shade. A sign warns NO CLIMBING: KEEP OFF. Still, every spring, wet tender leaves unfurl on branches jagged as broken bones, and the tree bursts out in a froth of white petals.

And every spring, the preachers line the sidewalk near the tree, and thrust their Bibles as we pass by. *Repent and be saved*, they say. *Turn or burn.* I want to tell them, *Turn around, turn around, and look at the tree*.

The day lays down

first summer heat as we drive
beyond Clarksdale through the Delta,

past cotton silos, Baptist graveyards,
little swamps with floating trash,

sometimes an egret. We turn on one-lane roads
leading past alfalfa fields

and a yellow crop duster gassing up,
getting ready to spray poison.

at the mississippi civil rights museum

—a golden shovel for Lucille Clifton: after "miss rosie"

1.

i am reading the names of the lynched when
the guard asks how i'm doing and i
start to cry. in one photo, crowds watch
a body burn, you
wouldn't believe their glee as the man is wrapped
in flame. a father in the picture lifts his boy up
on his shoulders. to the mob it is like
a holy war, they're *doin god's will, gettin garbage*
off the streets . . . now i am sitting
in one of the tiny film cubicles surrounded
by images from freedom summer, by
blown-up headlines about the missing men. it is 1964, the
bodies have been found, there's the smell
of death, legs poking from the mud, and deliquescing flesh of
two other boys found in the river during the search, too
long dead to identify. old
grief and guilt like a knobby rotten potato.

how the past peels
open when i see the photos or
hear the ringing freedom songs. when
the guard says kindly *if you want to talk*, i
can't talk, just flap my hand around . . . later i watch
a teacher with her students. *in this museum*, she says, *you*

will see what black people, and sometimes white, fought for here in
mississippi. the right to work, to learn, to vote. your
freedoms don't come cheap, she says, *for in the old*
days, the white man's
word was law. but how could we walk in the shoes
of the man who was lynched for "bringing suit," with
the man who was lynched for "hogging the road," with the
woman and her little
sons and daughter whose husband/father died because he
   wouldn't toe
the line? like mighty trees, cut
down. like holy flames, snuffed out.

i tell myself, *no more sitting.*
let me walk among those who fought and those still fighting,
   still waiting.

   2.

i think of your courage, lucille. for
in 1982, before that dignified white audience, you told how your
great-great-grandmother, the first lucille, was on your mind
the night you came to read at virginia. *not lynched in virginia like*
all the others, you told us, *but legally hanged because they*
   respected her. next
you said, *shot her baby's white father from his horse.* my week's
little concerns drained away, my papers to grade, the grocery
list, the cluttered house, and i saw the crossroads, i
saw dust and pines and broom sedge, heard clattering hooves,
   heard him say

for god's sake lucille don't. or maybe nothing at all. later, when
you came to my house for the reception, silent and shy i
sat on the steps, a scared new hire among the senior professors,
    eager just to watch
as they shook your hand, as you balanced your plate, saying
    goodby you
touched my cheek, told me, *your eyes are so radiant. i will
    remember you.*

3.

in the photos, jeering crowds surround protesters wet
with sweat and coke and catsup poured on their heads, their brown
and white faces grim at lunch counters. any pocket or bag
could hide a gun. i was the protesters' age but was not there, the
    summer of
burning churches. my mother was a
protective, cautious woman
who went to church, taught school, who
forbade me to go on the buses for freedom summer, who used
to say she'd die if i married "a negro." what is it like to
be a guard here, to comfort white women who weep, to be
surrounded each day by the history of suffering, the fire, the
    noose, the
prison whip called black annie that made scar-lace out of even
    the best-looking
back? not your grandma, not your mother, not your own sweet gal
was safe in mississippi. or in
arkansas, alabama, texas, louisiana, the carolinas, georgia.

what's it like to be a guard? to know that for stealing five pounds
   of ham they used
to give a black man ten years at parchman, then to
rent him out for convict labor until he'd starve, until he'd be
broken? yet in the darkest corners of parchman, freedom riders
   sang and called
on each other's courage, on the conscience and heart of the
nation. and you, lucille, paying homage to your own lost Georgia
Rose . . .
what was it like to be you? i
think of you with love. i stand
in this museum knowing that you lifted me up
and that you guide me still, through
what i have done and what i have failed to do. your
kindness, and the guard's, in the midst of so much cruelty,
   such destruction . . .
thinking of these, how can i
not take courage, how can i not stand
up?

Autumn Leaf, Yellow Raincoat

Whom can we turn to / in our need? Rilke asks in the First Duino Elegy
yesterday's street   some tree on a slope   O and the night,
the night when the wind full of worldspace / gnaws at our faces

I am sick of bamboo and wisteria thrusting their stubborn
    green outside my window
sick of gray lint packed into every crevice of my brain
    I want night   gnawing at my face

And I want the day when I walked with my love
    up a mountain outside Gstaad
my hair dyed Autumn Leaf   I wore my yellow raincoat

the ground was wet   a woman bounded down   followed
    by a poodle
who jumped up friendly and shook droplets   yes it was raining

and a few wild strawberries shone beside our feet
we climbed as far as the barn   the cattle trough
above us   the mountain   the clouds

Three

The Astonishing Light

—Written throughout November 2017
at Parchman, Mississippi State Penitentiary

Gray skies, this first day of November. Driving toward
the prison, we pass golden and brown pecan groves
and bales of cotton wrapped in yellow plastic,
lined up in rows along stubble fields. Scratches
of cotton still fleck the fields, fluffy white
on sharp stems. Birds rise in the distance.
Three huge farm trucks lumber along the narrow road.

When we get to Marks, we pass a high school team,
all Black, practicing in the rain. Prisoners
in green and white striped pants clear weeds,
pick up trash. We make this drive weekly,
Patrick and I, an hour and a half through the Delta
toward our students who are imprisoned
for anywhere from three years to life.

At Parchman we eat our lunch in a cracked
concrete parking lot across from the entrance,
a cheese sandwich for me, a hot meal for Patrick,
who prays before he eats. Then we enter the gates.

***

Now the 18,000 acres of Parchman Penitentiary,
around us in the middle of the Delta.

Beyond the entry, meager white houses dot the road,
where guards live with their families.
Outside some, a swing set or kids' bikes,
but no visible kids. Hallowe'en decorations—
a black plastic ogre, fake spiderwebs draped on bushes.

A tool building, more fences, bare fields, some tractors.
To the right, down a road we don't follow, the high walls
of maximum security. To the distant left, a low dark building
all by itself—Death Row, swarming with guard towers.

***

I see only what I see. Our tidy classroom building
with its dependable heat and AC,
the blackboard that Patrick covers with writing,
the semicircle of chairs, a green linoleum floor,
windows onto the fence with its coiled barbed wire.
Occasional flurries of little birds, back and forth
across the fence. Sparse grass, tiny blue daisies.
Across the parking lot, the windowless block
from which our students come, hurrying
through cold drizzle in their thin blue jackets
to our building—the windowless block
into which, every week, they vanish.

***

I'd like to know who our students are, how they
ended up here, what they'll do
once they're released. Sometimes they mention

their children, the wives or girlfriends
who wait for their return. I know enough about
Mississippi to know that they'll have trouble
finding work, but some were sentenced for no worse
than what the frat boys on my campus do at parties.

***

Today, watching bamboo sway in the dull
November rain outside my bedroom window,
I need to think about things other than
white supremacy, state-sanctioned premature death,
systemic undereducation, racial profiling,
the carceral state, the legacy of slavery —
the phrases Patrick uses when he speaks
of what we're fighting, our students'
ground down lives, and the way *Felon*
will follow them once they're out.

I am exhausted and angry and need to think
only about leaves thick on the ground,
a blue wintering sky, the tile roof
of the gleaming house next door.
And the gingko seedling I found in the hedge,
struggling for light amidst bamboo and wisteria.

***

Yesterday, a stinging rain. The windshield wipers
thwapped back and forth, but Patrick could hardly see
as we drove, talking about our students.

Let us learn to develop a dangerous unselfishness —
Patrick said King said that in his final sermon, in Memphis,
and when, not hearing, I asked, *Who?* Patrick said, *Martin King,*
and then he laughed, *My girlfriend always teases me I say*
Martin King like he was my best friend. He's on fire with King
and Malcolm X, Fannie Lou Hamer, Angela Davis,
all the narratives of slavery, prison, education, freedom.
Sometimes you can't change the confinement of your body,
he tells our students, *but you can free yourself*
from the confinement of your mind. He carries the word,
shakes the men's hands when they arrive, begins every class
with the chant that used to embarrass me, *I'M A STUDENT!*
I'M A TEACHER! I'M A SCHOLAR! I'M CREATIVE!—
we shout it three or four times together, and by now
I love how this affirmation revs up men to whom life has offered
little. Soon they are talking all at once. They tell us,
this class every week the one thing that get my mind going.

***

For me they write about romance, babies, football,
grandmas or aunties who raised them and pray for them,
cousins who died from guns, uncles who taught them
how to hunt and found them when they got lost in the woods.
Elaborate descriptions complete with maps of *Quick Bed,*
where they're sent first before being assigned in prison.
How the guys who aren't in gangs have to stand just so
at meal lines or they'll *get taken down,* how *security,*
which means gang members, guards the showers,
how two of the four toilets for sixty men are never working,
how it stinks. They describe being transferred from jail

to prison through the Mississippi night, in trucks fitted out
with divided kennels, one man to a side. They mention
taking the helicopter ride, but won't tell me what that means,
so I envision prisoners taken up one by one over the endless
acres of Parchman, just in case they thought they could escape.

***

One of our students is writing a book.
Forty-two years ago I shot a man who was
cheating me of overtime, and robbed him and fled.
When they caught me, I confessed. Turns out
he was high up in the Klan so they brought me
for my safety to Mississippi. Fourteen years ago,
he writes, he came up for parole, but his family
had all died and he had no place to go,
so they kept him here in prerelease.

I was a cradle Catholic, he writes.
They didn't bring me up to kill or steal.
I despaired of my soul until at last a priest came.
In all caps he letters out the passages, chapter
and verse, that he and the priest recited, back and forth,
like dueling Bibles, our student to prove damnation
and the priest to prove forgiveness, until at last,
in tears, our student accepted that even he
could be led through prayer to reconciliation.

Another man, too, is working on a book.
When I was five, he writes, *my baby brother*
choked on a pill. My daddy run through the door

screaming, pushing me out the way. Baby was blue.
I prayed with a glow on my face as if Jesus
was in the room with me, and the baby coughed
and lived. Later I lost God. — This is the part
he doesn't want to tell yet, how he ended up here.

But then in prison I signed up to work in the kitchen.
I met two men who taught me to cook
and they led me to the Bible. One told me,
See this bloody meat? What do that say to you?
I don't know, food poisoning? I answer.
O you child of little faith, he say, don't you know
the blood of Christ is here for you like always?

Now, our student says, *I pray without ceasing.*
Me and my people we serve the Lord.

***

Back home, the astonishing afternoon light.
Scarlet leaves of dogwoods and maples
grow brittle with umber, the small taste of death.

The astonishing light. These words I have written
haunt me. But to me, what do they mean?

***

Toward the end of our class today I looked out
across the barbed wire fence to a stubble field covered
with white birds. I said, *Oh look at the birds!* One man
told me they are cattle egrets and they come every night,

thousands of them, and settle in the field like a shining cloud.
Then as Patrick and I were leaving the building,
I asked the woman who works the front desk if she
had seen them and she replied, *My grandma always*
tell me a cloud of blackbirds mean cold weather coming.

I wondered why she said *black* until, as we drove away,
I looked up to see a sky filled with calligraphy—
lines intertwining, looping, angling off
and circling back, against the sunset. I watched them
for miles. These were the same birds, white in the light
of afternoon, dark against the roseate sky.

Four

The Teacher

The novelist and I picked our way down the trail,
bending double to duck under branches,
California drier than ever that summer,
pinecones thick on the ground, dust in our nostrils.
I hadn't talked to him much our first days
at the residency in the Santa Cruz Mountains,
but one afternoon he asked me to go hiking.
He said he'd never seen the trail
so snarled with underbrush, so thick the trees.
He had come here many times to write,
to watch the hawks and fog. He could still
run up the hill to the road but at 85 now,
guessed this might be the end of it.

I asked where he grew up. Złoczów, he told me,
a Polish town. When the deportations
started, a local teacher hid them.
His mother, two aunts, an uncle, himself,
silent while the students were downstairs.
When the attic grew dark, the teacher would come,
bringing just bread some days, other days thin soup,
a little sauerkraut or kale, a jug of water from the spring,
then leave as quickly as he'd come. *We knew him*
from town, he said. *My mother gave him jewelry—*
her sapphires, the brooch, the topaz necklace,
her gold and lapis bracelet —
not her wedding ring till near the end,

but everything she had.
            Then, after many years,
the teacher's grandson came to find him.
His wife served tea. The grandson
opened a small carved box, unrolled a cloth,
and laid the jewels before them. *Please,* he said,
I would not profit from your suffering.

So many questions I could not ask.
We climbed over a gate marked Private
and walked on to a chainlink fence
and the dogs, not hostile, but barking.

In winter, he continued, *the teacher took us*
from the attic and put us in a storeroom
so we would not freeze.
Huddled among old books, we lived in darkness.

We stood a long time watching the dogs.
Then we turned to retrace the trail,
back to the gate, along the flank of the mountain,
down the hill, to the house where others
and dinner awaited—salmon, farro, salad,
candlelight reflected in the plate glass windows,
linen napkins and quiet conversation.
As we sat over wine and coffee, fog spilled up from the sea.

Soon There Will Be More Unwanted Children

—italicized lines from Basho,
Travelogue of Weather-Beaten Bones

As fragile as the flowers
of bush-clover

that scatter at the slightest
stir of the autumn wind,

the abandoned child
by the Fuji River

reaches out wailing,
face streaked with mucus

and tears. Basho, moved
with pity, leaves food

but passes on. Here I stop.
Here I stop   each time.

Basho's footsteps fade
along the trail. He turns a corner.

Centuries pass, water
rushes over the stones,

chrysanthemums wither, leaves
fall and cover the little bones.

Owl

What does the day bring?
  —nothing

    When does the night end?
      —never

      Amid the dark trees
   the owl conjures her victims
    with her song

Costa Rica

1. *Pura Vida*

   —On study abroad at the ecolodge, 2015

Sweaty, dusty, in the morning sun,
we're helping to clear a field
for the tiny town of Upper San Luis
to celebrate their new Community Center.
Allie and Michael haul logs, thick as my thigh,
then toss them on the brush pile. Kendall and Maggie
wrap grasses and leaves in tattered canvas bags,
and carry them in bear hugs. Anne's in the underbrush,
raking. Cathy and I drag spikes of bamboo.
Two young men weed-eat one side of the field.
Hugo and his shy young wife tote brush
and gather sticks. Noah, straddled in a copse
of bamboo, slashes at trunks and branches,
diminishing trees, taking them down,
stopping only to sharpen his machete.

This handful of people halfway up a mountain
take time from their jobs to work together.
Bit by bit, the field—a snarl of scrubby trees,
bamboo, clotted grasses—gets cleared,
and the brush pile grows mountainous and sprawling.
The field will become a playground for the children,

an extension of the library, maybe even
a volleyball court. *Pura Vida*, locals greet us:
> May you be full of life.

Sweaty, dusty, scratched and bitten,
we gather in the Community Center for *horchata*,
apples, cookies. Someone goes to summon Noah,
who won't stop once he gets going.
Mostly we don't speak Spanish—except for Cathy,
who's Peruvian, and Anne, who lived in Ecuador.
But we grin. We grin and grin.

2.   Monteverde, a Zuihitsu

—Each night the wind, blanketing the Casa de Professor,
soughing, rushing, so strong it could knock you over

—each morning the rain, bedewing my hair

—honey-colored cows the night we arrived, nosing the
windows of our van, the farmer guiding them to the fields
through the dark along the rutted mountain roads, and
Mary waking, staring outside, muttering, "This is the best
night of my whole life ever"

—Oscar our guide at the cloud forest, his excitement hearing,
then finding, a three-wattled bellbird, its brown belly and
white head, through the binoculars, white triple wattles dangling

—on the midnight guided walk, piercing darkness, then like a fever dream, a knee-high flashlit cave filled with hundreds of tiny white spiders

—enormous strangler figs, the channels and ropy sinews of their trunks where they grew up and around and choked the trees, sky-high and sinuous

—a hummingbird's tiny head poking up above its nest, and the long needle-like beak, glimpsed through binoculars under a clump of moss high in a tree, Oscar knew just where to look for it

—the leafcutter ant that ate a hole in my bamboo sock, and Oscar telling us that, in the past, leafcutter ants were used to stitch shut wounds because you could pull their bodies off and their jaws, clamped shut, remained

—the injured coati that crossed our path, patterned fur, the long prehensile tail

—Allie, with her masses of curly black hair and her habit of saying, "I'm sorry, I'm sorry"

—Michael and Anne playing soccer in a twilit mountain field with the little son of Christina, who made us *arepas* for our "cook in a home" tour

—stale chocolate truffles urged upon us overpriced on our "small scale local chocolate" tour

—semi-loneliness of being more than twice the age of all my students, as they all became closer to each other they chattered and chattered and naturally enough they did not include me

—missing Peter, especially at night, to keep me warm

—lichen stick bug

—female quetzal

—the urge to write my name on a tree because we pass, we pass, we will never be here again, *yo soy, yo soy*, I am the one who is alive right now, and here right now, and then not here, though the tree remains

—our guide Miguel at the Butterfly Garden, his Sanskrit sutra tat *May all beings be happy may all beings be at peace*, if I were young I would get tattoos—and Miguel holding a lacewing butterfly gently between his fingers

—the waterfall at the end of the trail—still there, always there, a type of heaven, a type of eternity, always changing, always the same, in the midst of a cloud forest, with mist and life beyond life, intertangled, always dying, always growing

—dreaming, the final night, that I found a hummingbird's nest attached to the juncture of two flowering branches—the flowers tiny, bluish purple—in the nest, a broken egg, a few ants circling

—dreaming I climbed the stairs to the plane with the nest still in my hand

—the wind, still blowing, always blowing

Now and Again

—in the California mountains

Stars litter the mown ditches, blown from thistles.
The fawns' spots fade with latening June.
The morning glory's like thimbles of milk
among seed-heavy grasses
where a thousand thousand weed stems
arc and angle without words.

A red-tailed hawk rides the thermals, hovering.

I have a death to bring you,
but now and again I return to live oak forests
and fields dropping off through fog
toward the ocean
and cries of birds in twilight
and wind blowing where it pleases.

Letters to My Sister

The Robin

In the final photograph of you, you reach up to cup your friend's shoulder. She has taken a ferry, then two planes, and traveled a night and a day to come to you. The light through the great-rooted oak outside your window makes your nightgown rosy and the bedroom full of shadows. You are so frail you've practically vanished. Like the baby robin we found on the sidewalk in Camp Hill when we were small.

~

The Wood

We're not weeping people. We don't fall out, don't cling to each other. But when suddenly I noticed the rough wooden cart outside the door at the back of the chapel, and on it, a coffin, oh, that was the worst, I hadn't realized you'd be present at your funeral. It was okay as long as you were absent—but this, your *present* absence—your body wrapped, I had been told, in the pale pink linen robe Josh ironed with such love and grief for you, right there, so close—Then they wheeled the coffin forward and I came and stood beside it, to speak of you. I put my hand on the wood, as if I could touch you—

~

Smoocher Gommers

Today, ahead of stormy weather, Bruce picked irises and drove them to your grave. He texted, *I'll be like the old men in the movies—I'll talk to her, tell her what I've been doing.* I texted back, *I've been missing her so much. Tell her smoocher gommers.*

Trouble is, I don't remember what that meant. You would remember, J.

~

If I Drove to St. Louis
you would not come to the kitchen door and stand at the top of the porch steps to greet me. You would not have made pozole so I could eat when I arrived. Your kitchen would not be redolent of hominy and ham.

I never told you that, when we were kids and you started bleeding, I found the underwear you had buried in your closet. Under a pile of clothes, three pairs of JCPenney underpants: the crusted stains. I was shocked, but now I rejoice in you, sweet sister—your privacy, your weirdness.

You yelled at me when I borrowed your clothes and stank them up with cigarettes. In revenge, I locked you out when my friend came over, and you slammed the door to your room and cried. If I could open the door and let you sit on my bed, I would.

~

What Remains
I have lost you — you, who ate vegetables and climbed mountains, who never smoked and lived so much healthier than I. And I've spent so much time being sad. It's easier than running my hand along the tough sinew of the actual.

Wind rises in the pecan trees, and the sun glints through the interstices of leaves. A robin disappears into the forsythia.

Across the street, our immaculate neighbor wanders around his yard, plucking infinitesimal weeds.

I keep your picture on top of the pile of books by my bed. You are in Paris, at a café, maybe fifteen years ago, holding a newspaper open. Short blonde hair, sunglasses, tank top, strong shoulders. You are reading, lost in the intricate maze of your thoughts. Never did you look more beautiful.

Thum

How many hours
   have I spent on this porch,
      idly stroking my thumb,
    where the trees
join overhead and mingle
   their enormous swaying branches.
       I want to lie down, my sister said,
    I do not want to eat,
though her husband and I kept coaxing her
   try just half a hemp gummy
      in our desperate wish
    that her appetite
would magically revive.
   That night she and I watched
      The Great British Baking Show,
    second time for both of us,
we sat on the white couch
   with her head on my shoulder,
      and once again the Indian guy
    we liked, who found his tray
too heavy, took first prize.
   Next morning as her husband
      drove me to the airport,
    I asked to stop so I could buy
her flowers. I wrote, *I love you*
   always, and the card stayed
      on their windowsill for weeks

after she died. Tonight I'm
remembering Thum, vile liquid painted on our thumbs
when we were small,
                    to make us quit before
we joined our father,
who was stationed in Japan. It tasted bitter,
        but bit by bit I'd take it on my tongue
                    until it wore away,
            the bitterness nearly pleasing.
I'm thinking about the strangeness of time,
        what fades, what stays—
                        back then the two small girls
            curled up beneath the covers
singing lullabies to each other—
        one now buried in pale linen
                    on a bed of flowers
                in an Amish coffin,
the other possessed
        by a nightly dance.
                        When I lie down
            the cramps begin,
first in the arches of my feet,
            then in my ankles, which torque
                    and writhe,
            and on up until my legs are rigid.
If I can breathe beneath the current
        of agony, sink down beneath
                        the agitated waves,
            at last the cramps subside.
—And why am I telling you this?

The dance of all this dying,
                    all this grieving,
           all this pain, seems to me
like *prana* moving through us,
        like those swaying branches
                  in midsummer,
            Mississippi, where at night
the vast trees throb with cicadas' silver music.

The Wanderer

—after Andreas Rentsch's video piece

The loneliest man wanders through crosshatched
        thorns at the edge of night
is there a path there? where the sudden slash of light is?
          is he the hunted or the hunter
looming in the moonlight
            larger for the way the darkness falls upon him?

he is not dangerous though you may wish him so
      for then he could fit all your nightmares
                    look
how the moon rises   between the blackened trees
as if
to guide him

now he is running again
through the stubble field   Joe Christmas
      or fleeing the flame thrower
         jumping the ditch
             saluting
the unseen that follows him   look
     he throws his arms up

defiant blest cursed wanderer you wear history
        stand and confront them   find peace
in the shattered moonlight

Wooden Comb

I want to go into a far country,

get away from this knowing, rediscover
light on the water and the odor of thyme

sun warmed and acrid on the hillside. To go,
with him, to find that stone hut

on a trail outside Campouriez, where we walked
one long ago midnight away from the village

to watch moonrise across the mountains—
that abandoned one-room hut where a woman,

I imagined, once combed her hair with a wooden comb.
My heart has grown numb. Today, buttercups blossom

in the muddy fields, along the parking strips
all over town, and my students calmly discuss

what forms of life will exist beyond apocalypse.
I cannot reconcile how the world is sweet,

how the world is burning. Next door
in the trees a little bird is chipping at the night.

Five

Of the Eternal Waters

I don't care
if you saved a little boy
by grabbing the tail of his shirt
as he was falling off a Ferris wheel
or performed a Heimlich
as Danny choked on chicken
or tucked your feet behind your neck
and balanced on your hands
or if you loved to snuggle
with your blue-eyed roundish mother
or you loved your Army father
but couldn't make his slide rule work
or you wish you had a parrot
who said *timor mortis conturbat me*
or you wish you had an Airedale
or you wish you had a kitten
or your son painted your bedroom
it's like sleeping in a daffodil
or your apple pie's to die for
or you once ate a pansy
and mustard and potato chips
and applesauce on tuna
or you dream you could wander
on every glorious *Wanderweg*
in the flower-speckled Alps
or your irises are blooming
or your salvias are blooming

or something ate your basil
or Van Gogh, Magritte, and Brueghel
or one night by the Seine
or one noon in the café
or you love his warm, blunt hands
or fire glints off your opal ring
or you've taught here thirty years
or your smile could charm a badger
you can't wade in this fountain

Transformations

And insects in the midnight trees and grasses, their stridulations
        making the dark shimmer.
Beyond the willow oak, beyond the Osage orange and thicket
        of bamboo, an owl, its hollow call, then the shriek
        and skitter of the small terrified creature
caught mid-scream
dangling from its claws, rising from the field right by my window
        as we drove past.

Even that. Or when we leaned against each other sleepless,
        after wandering all night in Iraklion
from our cinderblock hotel to the fortress, the pier, where we watched
        the ocean lap the stones, and back to town—
        leaned against each other at dawn at the open-air market,
groggy, gazing at the butcher,
how he wielded saw and cleaver, his apron covered with blood,
        and seeing us transfixed, asked were you a butcher in America.

Immolation—I hid among the stacks of the Army library
        at Camp Zama, Japan, age ten, to read a children's book
        about the girl from Domrémy called
Joan. I wanted it bad, because then God would speak to me, I would
kindle in his care, caught in
light, a dart of flame. When I was small, I swore angels walked
        beneath the trees, angels wandered in the garden,
        all the dust motes in the window were angels.

Mother, may I? Father, sisters, may I? Oak leaves, gingko leaves
        lie brittle on the sidewalk. I count my dead
        in the hollow twilight.
Nights, sometimes, I can almost touch them.

Oh my love, my darling, I hunger for your touch . . .
        not a long lonely time, though. We lie spoons
        in our heart pine house—
pine beams so dense with sap that termites couldn't chew
        all the way through.
Quick! I called you that day, watching the swallows
        swoop through the trees,
rising and swirling,
swear to God they were beautiful. And now,
this scarred, aging body devouring itself, can I praise my destroyer,
        knowing walls, house, great-leaved trees, all those I love,
        like myself will vanish?

Under the covers, hiding when I was small, afraid of what I'd heard
        about Nazis. If I had to choose my mother or my father,
        which would I choose?
Vowed I'd choose myself: take me.
What then? What, as we edge closer to the
X, the crossroads, in the Heraclitean fire where all things
        blaze and dwindle—
you, me, the feathered silvery seeds of grasses, bulrushes
        bursting with seed, late October asters and daisies,
        mottled red sweet gum leaves, black-eyed Susans,
year's last
zinnias?

Pecans

In the slant of late afternoon light,
hundreds of pecans stand out tawny against
the mud, fallen leaves, matted grass,
and I can't stop drifting around the yard
stuffing them in my pockets. This is a gift
November in Mississippi offers after a freeze.
If they release from the husk they will be good,
if they cling they will be rotten or wormy,
and I learn to discern the barely perceptible
difference in weight between plump and desiccate.
Last night's wind took down some branches.
Maybe someday this old tree will
come down and kill us. We exist by grace
or chance in the free fall of every moment,
but for now, my life is full of sweetness, pecans
like little brains tucked in their bitter shells.

...

Yesterday, in the Batesville Feed and Seed
that advertises *We Crack Your Pecans*,
the smell of overripe tomatoes, pesticides
and herbicides, corroded bottles of medicine
for hoof rot and mange and lord knows what else,
climbed up my nostrils and wouldn't let go.
A couple of old guys lounged on wooden chairs.
Customers came and went, asking about

pumpkins (none) and pecans (sold out).
Decades of dust webbed the farm tools,
furred the boxes of Miracle Gro and snail bait,
spidered above the rusty stand of seed packets—
spinach, collard greens, dahlias. Nine baby chicks
pecked grain in a warm-lit cage
at the back of the store. We wandered the aisles,
ducking outside from time to time for air,
to the "Garden Center" with its few six-packs
of dead marigolds and salvia. In the adjacent
concrete workspace, the huge pecan-cracker
clackety-clacked and the blower blew the chaff off.

. . .

Now, back home, we have picked through
28 pounds of pecans, separated stray bits
of shell from the meat, discarded rotten
or shriveled nuts, broken off blackened
corners, carefully nudged the bitter central
membrane from the sweet flesh halves,
and filled gallon bags with the plump fruit
of my November hours and hours wandering
over the yard, my nearsighted gaze
fixed to discern the tawny oblong shells
from among leaves and sticks and grass.
We have gleaned this year's harvest
from the enormous, gnarly, messy-leafed tree
whose shade in summer stretches far across
the lawn and over the driveway.

Five fat worms curl blind and maggot-like
among the litter at the bottom of the bucket.
High in the branches, a few remaining
husks hang, open, dark, like agitated stars.

Visitation

Now the gray descends
over wet streets,
patches of snow, the new
quiet of an empty house.

Rosy and round as
Shmoos in their fleece-lined Christmas Comfies,
the grandchildren have left. I will not see them
until buttercups, clover,

violets, speckle the grass now
waste with winter, and the little
x-es of spearlike leaves. Over time
you'd think it would hurt less, but there's always a

zero . . .
and then the car turns the corner. I breathe.
Beds need making, floors need sweeping,
clothes need washing, toys need putting away.

Dailiness carries me, the small blessings of work
exhaust me, and evening comes.
"Family," Bodhi said, "I like that part best in *Coco*.
Ghosts and skeletons are my friends."

He's four. He tells me,
"I made the world so I'll help you with the ghosts.

Just tell them you want to be their friend.
Kiss them. And then they need to be fed."

Love holds me together with them.
Months, miles, cannot diminish it.

And Troops Massed at the Borders

I was alive while the nations killed the earth.
Love grew thin on my tongue.
Mostly I kept to my own small life.
Not that I didn't care, but
what could I do, when greed and
pride gnashed at the flesh of the world?

Quince blossoms made it through the freeze,
rose pink on thorny branches,
a pleasure, a comfort, and cardinals warbling
under the blanket of evening sky—Then a skein,
a V of geese crying southward overhead, lit up
where the sun gilded their bellies. What matter,
I thought sometimes, if we X each other out,
the human race, we don't deserve this beauty.

Day Without Number

You must go to the valley of ashes
and find there the woman
with the wooden comb.
She will tell you what to do.
If you leave now you may travel safely.
The birds have stopped singing.
The black cat no longer scratches at the window.
Set out on the road that stretches
back to the milk, the simple bowl,
the starless night that gathers around you.
What might she tell you, this woman?
She might say, I was once like you.
I lived between thistles and honey,
far from the village, alone on the mountain.
What happened? nothing happened.
I have settled into peace.
You too will sleep when hope and fear are gone.

Milagro of a Sacred Heart and Three Beech Leaves, Each Mottled with Green and Crimson

Now the silverfish have eaten your sad dictionary.
Once you stood behind the counter,

ribbons in your hair, you measured and cut yardage
for the buxom ladies. And now a pile of Kleenex

rises by your elbow as you cope with your rhinitis.
You have become the remnants bin, hair lank

and thinning, nails blue with cyanosis.
It baffles you, doesn't it?—how in the junkyard

of the heart, those hours, those days, still shine—
the week in the little fishing village, tables

on the sand, the anchovies and gardenias.
All gone, all gone. And now the mottled leaves.

But I tell you, you're no minimum.
You're peaches so tender they bruise

where they touch the sassafras bowl.
You're silver-olive lichen on the willow oak tree,

moss between the bricks. Sweet ripening figs,
small turtle hiding in the grass, green field

and green ephemera. All these things are you.
And the click and weave of birdsong after rain.

Jagged Paradise

Zing!
You're alive, aren't you?
X-rays show nothing wrong,
why fight against this happiness?
—violets clustering between the bricks on the front walk,
under the pecan tree, spider lilies intricate and scarlet,
Theo the tuxedo cat lapping cream on the porch.

~

Sunlight on the trail this morning warms my love's neck
    and his worn
red shirt—it gilds the bulrushes, silvers the feathery grasses.
Quick, look! as we walk, the heron who lives by the little
pond rises heavy-bodied into the trees.
One rudbeckia, one purple zinnia,
not much else grows where the trail branches off into darkness.

~

Moon tonight is full, sailing around the sky, clouds whipping past.
Leaning on my husband, I crook my neck to look up at the sky.
Keep him safe, moon and sky, keep him in your care, my guy in his
jeans and hiking boots, his olive-colored shirt and the belt
    tongue that keeps curling.
In my squeaky voice I sing him *Il y a longtemps que je t'aime*.
How old we're growing together, him with his toenails sharp
    as knives,
gnarly eyebrows, me with my twisted toes. We love the
    things we love
for what they are, wrote Frost, and it's true.

~

Every cicada sings us closer to winter now,

darkness soaks the grasses, pools beneath the trees.

Come here, little one, whoever you may be, the day and
    night ripen

blood red berries of sumac, dogwood, roses.

All the leaves are mottled and stained. Amen. Breathe in,
    it's late October.

Amulet

After you are gone
                    the fog will flow
                                      across these hills
where the barn swallow's breast
                        will shimmer of peaches

After you too
                    are nothing but crumble and sliver
                                  the swallows
will celebrate the sky
                            buttercups and poppies
flaunt their fiery tongues
                    and the bobcat suckle
                            her needle-clawed cubs
in secret fur-lined caves
                        beneath the trees

Before you were as after you will be

Thich Nhat Hanh, or Thay

The quality of mercy is not strained;
It droppeth as the gentle rain from heaven
—Shakespeare, *The Merchant of Venice*

Rain taps the walls gently,
pock   pock   pock,   then slides to the deck,
filling this gray morning
where I lie beside my husband in our bed,
warm and new from sleep.

It soaks the shining mosses,
makes the resurrection ferns grow plump again,
and I am thinking of Thay,
whose funeral rites I watched,
livestreamed from Hue,

Thay, Beloved Teacher, whose face
as he lay on his bier
held such gentleness, whose monks and nuns
in saffron robes vivid as marigolds
filled the meditation halls

and bowed in quiet prostrations,
the struck, vibrating singing bowl
calling us each time
back to the breath. I sat breathing,
watching, as in a vast procession

chosen ones dressed in gold and scarlet
carried his casket heaped with chrysanthemums
to the fire, and I thought, *How could I ever*
be afraid of death?
                    This morning I woke
still wrapped in his blessing, merciful as the rain.

Acknowledgments

My thanks to the journals in which these poems first appeared, often in different forms or with different titles.

About Place Journal: "The Astonishing Light," "And Troops Massed at the Borders"

Crab Creek Review: "Fraught Season"

Cutthroat: "Letters to My Sister"

EcoTheo Review: "Thum"

Klimaaksjon /Norwegian Writers' Climate Campaign / NWCC: "Winter Day on the Whirlpool Trails"

Mantis: "Catalpa," "Winter Day on the Whirlpool Trails"

Marsh Hawk Review: "Imagining Caroline Casper. Nebraska 1880," "The Wanderer"

NELLE: "Postcard of an Anonymous Wooden Carving"

Orion: "Milagro of a Sacred Heart and Three Beech Leaves, Each Mottled with Green and Crimson"

Persimmon Tree: "Inhabitation," "Soon There Will Be More Unwanted Children"

Plant-Human Quarterly: "Pecans"

Quartet Journal: "And Behind Us, Only Air"

RockPaperPoem: "Autumn Leaf, Yellow Raincoat"

Shenandoah: "Persimmons"

Southern Humanities Review: "at the mississippi civil rights museum"

Terrain.org: "A Young Stag at Dusk"

Thalia Magazine: "Meditation Facing into Rain," "Wooden Comb"

The Ilanot Review: "Ironing," "Outside Sagamihara"

Valparaiso Poetry Review: "Late May"

"Catalpa" and "Winter Day on the Whirlpool Trails" were published in *Poetry and Science: Writing Our Way to Discovery*," ed. Lucille Lang Day (Scarlet Tanager Press, 2021).

"I Want to Be a Gladiola" and "Of the Eternal Waters" were published in *The Strategic Poet: Honing the Craft*, ed. Diane Lockward (Terrapin Books, 2021).

"Namesake" was published in *Community of Writers Written Here and There 2020 Anthology*, eds. Jill Bergantz and Neysa King.

"The day lays down" and "Pecans" were published in *Dispatches from the Poetry Wars*: *Poetics for the More-than-Human World: An*

Anthology of Poetry and Commentary, eds. Mary Newell, Bernard Quetchenbach, and Sarah Nolan (Spuyten Duyvil Press, 2020).

Letterpress prints of "Winter Day on the Whirlpool Trails" and "Catalpa" were exhibited with paintings by Barbara Howey under the title "Damage Poison Beauty Ooze," September 2017, in the symposium *In the Open*, LAND2, University of Sheffield, England.

Many people helped this book become what it is. My online writing group—Wendy Taylor Carlisle, Ana Doina, Iris Jamahl Dunkle, Patricia Fargnoli (now deceased), Ann Hofstetler, Louisa Howerow, Athena Kildegaard, Alicia Ostriker, Penelope Scambly Schott, Barbara Taylor, Sam Wilder—read and critiqued drafts of most of these poems over the years, and Alicia Ostriker gave me helpful feedback on the entire manuscript in its next-to-final iteration. Wendy Taylor Carlisle, Beth Ann Fennelly, and Jennifer Key, early on, and Melissa Ginsburg, toward the end, gave it their scrupulous, brilliant attention. My deep thanks to them all. And to my husband, Peter Wirth, for suggestions that greatly improved several poems—and, as always, for his encouragement and faith in my work.

Special thanks to Kathryn Hood for her wisdom and friendship.

I am grateful to the Black Earth Institute, of which I am a senior fellow, for its support and welcoming community over the years. Also I'm grateful to the Community of

Writers Poetry Workshop at Olympic Valley, California; the workshop leaders and my fellow poets welcomed and critiqued several of these poems in 2020.

This work is generously supported by funding from the Mississippi Arts Commission, a state agency, and in part, from the National Endowment for the Arts, a federal agency. All my thanks to MAC.

Thank you to the various editors who published poems as they came into being, and especially to Diane Lockward, who selected *Paradise Is Jagged* for the Redux series. I am delighted and proud to be part of Terrapin Books.

So much love to my birth family, now all gone, and to my present family — my husband, children, sons-in-law, and grandchildren. This book is for them and for the earth. Most of all, it is for Jennifer.

About the Author

Ann Fisher-Wirth is the author of six previous books of poetry, including *The Bones of Winter Birds* (Terrapin Books, 2019) and *Mississippi*, a poetry/photography collaboration with Maude Schuyler Clay (Wings Press, 2018). With Laura-Gray Street, she coedited *The Ecopoetry Anthology* (Trinity UP, 2013). She is the recipient of a 2023 Governor's Award for Excellence in Literature awarded by the Mississippi Arts Commission. Other awards include three Mississippi Arts Commission Poetry Fellowships and the Mississippi Institute of Arts and Letters Poetry Prize. She has had residencies at Djerassi, Hedgebrook, The Mesa Refuge, Camac/France, and Storyknife, and was the 2017 Anne Spencer Poet in Residence at Randolph College. In 1994-1995 she taught on a Fulbright award at Fribourg, Switzerland, and in 2002-2003 she was the Fulbright Distinguished Chair of American Studies at Uppsala, Sweden. Recently she co-edited a collection of eco-writing and eco-art from Africa, Asia, Latin America, Oceania, and the American South with Laura-Gray Street and regional editors Mildred Barya, Esther Vincent, Juan Carlos Galeano, and Craig Santos Perez, for the journal *The Global South*. A senior fellow and board member of the Black Earth Institute, she is recently retired from the University of Mississippi, where she taught in the MFA program and directed the Environmental Studies program. She lives in Oxford, Mississippi.

www.annfisherwirth.com

CPSIA information can be obtained
at www.ICGtesting.com
Printed in the USA
BVHW071023230123
656884BV00018B/161

9 781947 896604